Jesus in Space

Jesus in Space

A True Story That's Out of This World

Written by Cecilia Cicone

Illustrated by Gabhor Utomo

Pauline
BOOKS & MEDIA

Library of Congress Cataloging-in-Publication Data

ISBN 0-8198-4042-4

ISBN 978-0-8198-4042-4

Cover art by Gabhor Utomo

Photos on pages 25–27 are from NASA. Photos of astronauts used with permission.

Published by Pauline Books & Media, 50 Saint Pauls Avenue, Boston, MA 02130-3491

Printed in Korea

JIS SIPSKOGUNKYO4-2098 4042-4

www.pauline.org

Pauline Books & Media is the publishing house of the Daughters of St. Paul, an international congregation of women religious serving the Church with the communications media.

2 3 4 5 6 7 8 9 28 27 26 25 24

For Sr. Allison Regina and Sr. Orianne Pietra René,
thank you for always encouraging my crazy ideas for the glory of God.

Tom was an astronaut. He trained to go to space, and he ate space food. There was only one problem. Tom hadn't been to space yet!

NASA

JANUARY 16, 1990: Dr. Tom Jones is selected to join the next astronaut class for NASA.

He worked very hard to prepare for the day when he would finally go on a mission. Tom spent long hours flying airplanes, taking classes, and learning how to operate the space shuttle. He wore his space suit in a special swimming pool to feel weightless, just like he would be in space.

Then, the day came that Tom had been hoping for.

JULY 16, 1990: Dr. Tom Jones begins training as an astronaut candidate with his class. They practice flying, experience zero gravity, scuba dive, and study about space.

"Tom, we have a special mission for you," the astronaut director told him. "We need you to be a part of a team of astronauts who will take new and detailed pictures of the Earth from space. The photographs will help us understand forests, mountains, and seasonal changes on the Earth. They will make it easier to study events like volcano eruptions and earthquakes, to help keep people safe. Would you like to be on this team?"

JULY 16, 1991: Dr. Tom Jones finishes his year of astronaut training.

Immediately, Tom felt joyful. He would now have a chance to use the gifts God had given him to help people.

"Yes, of course!" Tom replied.

"Thank you for taking this job," his boss said. "You will have some time to train and prepare. The mission will not be easy, but I know you are the right person for the job."

As Tom left the meeting, he nearly floated down the hall! He whispered this prayer, "Thank you, Jesus."

FEBRUARY 1992: Dr. Tom Jones is asked to join the crew of STS-59, a mission aboard the space shuttle *Endeavour*. "STS" stands for "Space Transportation System."

The next two years were busy for Tom. He met the other astronauts who would make up the crew. They spent nearly every workday together. They planned their spaceflight. They practiced what to do if something went wrong. And they got to know each other better so that they could work well together and help each other.

MARCH 5, 1993: The entire crew of STS-59 begins training together. The crew includes Sidney Gutierrez, Kevin Chilton, Jay Apt, Michael Clifford, Linda Godwin, and Tom Jones.

Even though training was busy, Tom made sure to pray every day and to go to Mass with his family every Sunday. Each week, he walked into church and knelt down facing the gold box in the front. This box, called a tabernacle, held Jesus, who is truly present in the Eucharist. "Jesus, strengthen me for this week ahead," he prayed, "I cannot do this without you." After receiving Jesus in Holy Communion, Tom knelt in the pew. "Thank you for being so close to me, inside me and with me, Jesus." He always left church knowing that he was not alone. Tom knew that God would be going on this mission with him.

One day, the commander made an announcement: "We're going camping! When we are in space, we will be in our small ship and home will be far away. Camping will be good practice for living and working as a team."

Everyone agreed.

OCTOBER 22, 1993: The crew goes camping at Brazos Bend State Park in Houston to prepare for their mission.

One night around a campfire, they shared how excited they were for the mission. "I can't wait to see what Earth looks like from space!" one astronaut said.

"It will be pretty amazing to float weightless around the cabin," another one said.

The astronauts talked about the hard work ahead and took turns teaching each other some of the skills they would need in space. They spoke about the real dangers of going up there.

Tom's commander, Sid, said, "We're going to be in space for nine days. Can we find a way to receive Jesus in the Holy Eucharist in space?"

The pilot, named Kevin, smiled. "I have an idea," he said. "You don't need to worry."

DECEMBER 3, 1993: Dr. Tom Jones goes for a ride on the centrifuge, a flight simulator. The astronauts experience what it feels like to be pushed back into their seats when the space shuttle launches.

FEBRUARY 25, 1994: The crew of STS-59 goes into the cabin of *Endeavour* for the first time to test their flight systems.

MARCH 2, 1994: Dr. Tom Jones tests out his astronaut spacesuit for the first time.

MARCH 19, 1994: The space shuttle *Endeavour* goes out to the launchpad to be prepared for liftoff.

MARCH 31, 1994: Dr. Tom Jones and the rest of the crew are quarantined to make sure that they are healthy before going into space together.

Soon, the big day came. The astronauts climbed aboard a special bus called the Astrovan and rode out to the launchpad, where the space shuttle waited to take them into orbit.

APRIL 8, 1994: The launch of the space shuttle is delayed due to wind.

The time ticked on until finally the crew's family and friends were hearing the countdown every second. "T-minus five . . . four . . . three . . . two . . ."

Shuttle *Endeavour*'s engines roared to life. This was it! "Jesus, I trust in you!" Tom prayed.

APRIL 9, 1994, at 7:05 a.m. (EDT): Astronaut Tom Jones and the crew launch into low Earth orbit from John F. Kennedy Space Center in Florida.

The big booster rockets lit up with a tremendous crash. The astronauts were pushed into the backs of their seats as the rocket fuel propelled them out of the Earth's atmosphere. They were headed into space!

APRIL 9, 1994, at 7:13 a.m. (EDT): The main engines of *Endeavour* are cut off as the space shuttle nears Earth orbit.

In less than nine minutes, they were circling the Earth in orbit. The astronauts unstrapped and moved out of their seats to go to work.

APRIL 9, 1994, at 7:42 a.m. (EST): The maneuvering engines of *Endeavour* are shut down, placing the crew into Earth orbit for their science mission. Earth's gravity keeps *Endeavour* circling the Earth. The crew will orbit the Earth for eleven days.

Each of the astronauts had a different job so that the mission would be a success. The radar camera could take high-quality pictures of our changing planet, 120 miles below. Scientists on Earth would use the pictures to measure farmland moisture and map earthquake lines. They could also track ocean pollution and changes in dangerous volcanoes. The astronauts kept the camera working twenty-four hours a day in space. They took turns sleeping.

APRIL 9–18, 1994: The astronauts complete the work of this mission, taking detailed radar images of our changing Earth from space.

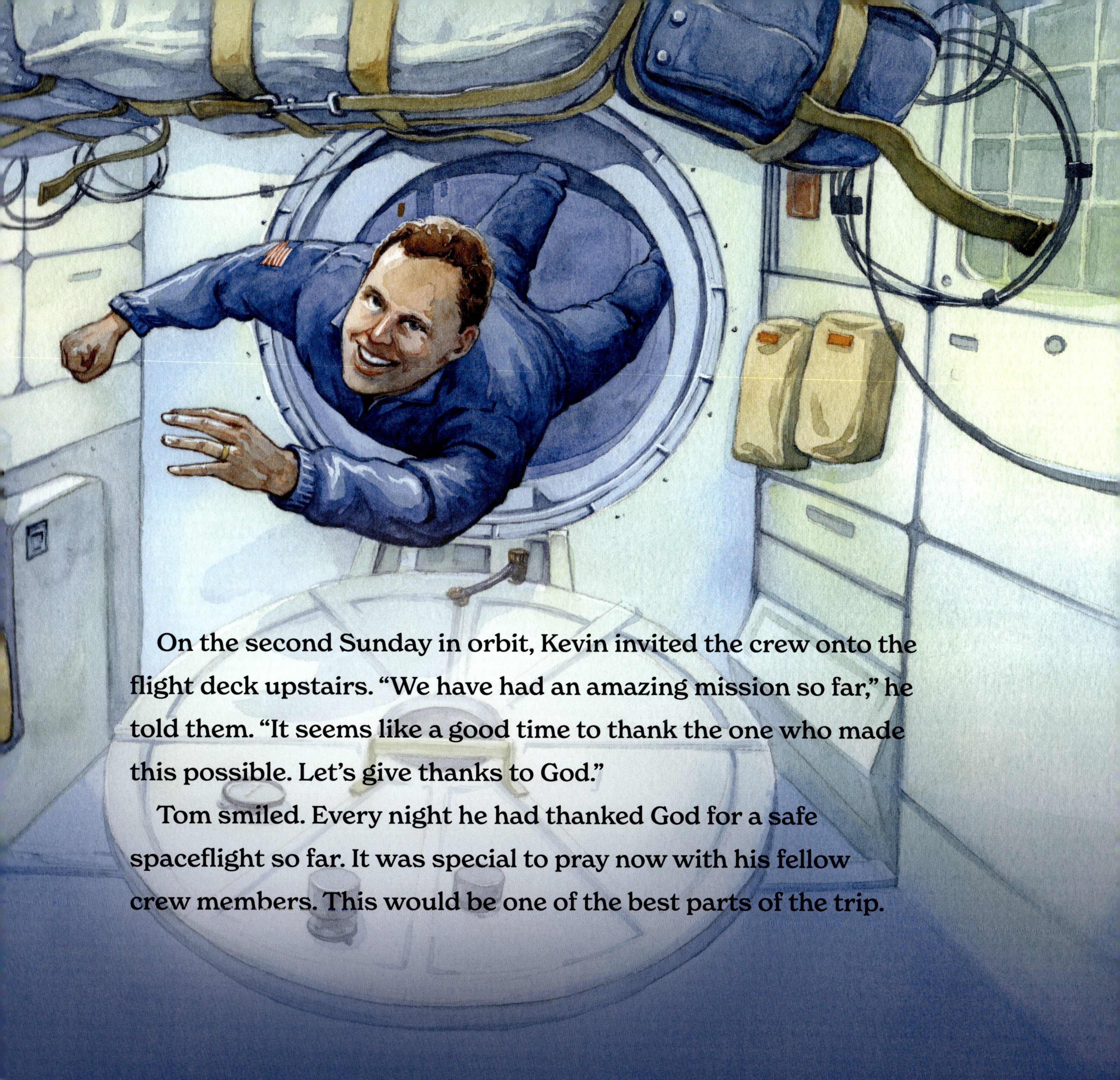

On the second Sunday in orbit, Kevin invited the crew onto the flight deck upstairs. "We have had an amazing mission so far," he told them. "It seems like a good time to thank the one who made this possible. Let's give thanks to God."

Tom smiled. Every night he had thanked God for a safe spaceflight so far. It was special to pray now with his fellow crew members. This would be one of the best parts of the trip.

They were orbiting around the night side of the Earth and it was dark except for a few lights coming from the instruments.

Kevin said, "I am what is called an Extraordinary Minister of Holy Communion. Sometimes a priest cannot bring the Eucharist to Catholics unable to go to Mass. He gives the Eucharist to me so that I can bring Jesus to them. I have this little gold container, called a pyx. There is one Eucharistic Host inside it for each of us."

They took turns reading from the Bible to hear God's words to them.

APRIL 17, 1994: Astronauts Tom Jones, Kevin Chilton, and Sidney Gutierrez receive Holy Communion on the Second Sunday after Easter while orbiting the Earth.

Then, Kevin took the Eucharist out of the pyx and said, "Body of Christ," to the Catholic astronauts one by one. They each replied, "Amen," and received Holy Communion. Suddenly, the sun started to shine through the windows of the flight deck. The brilliant sunlight brought tears to Tom's eyes and made the cockpit bright and warm.

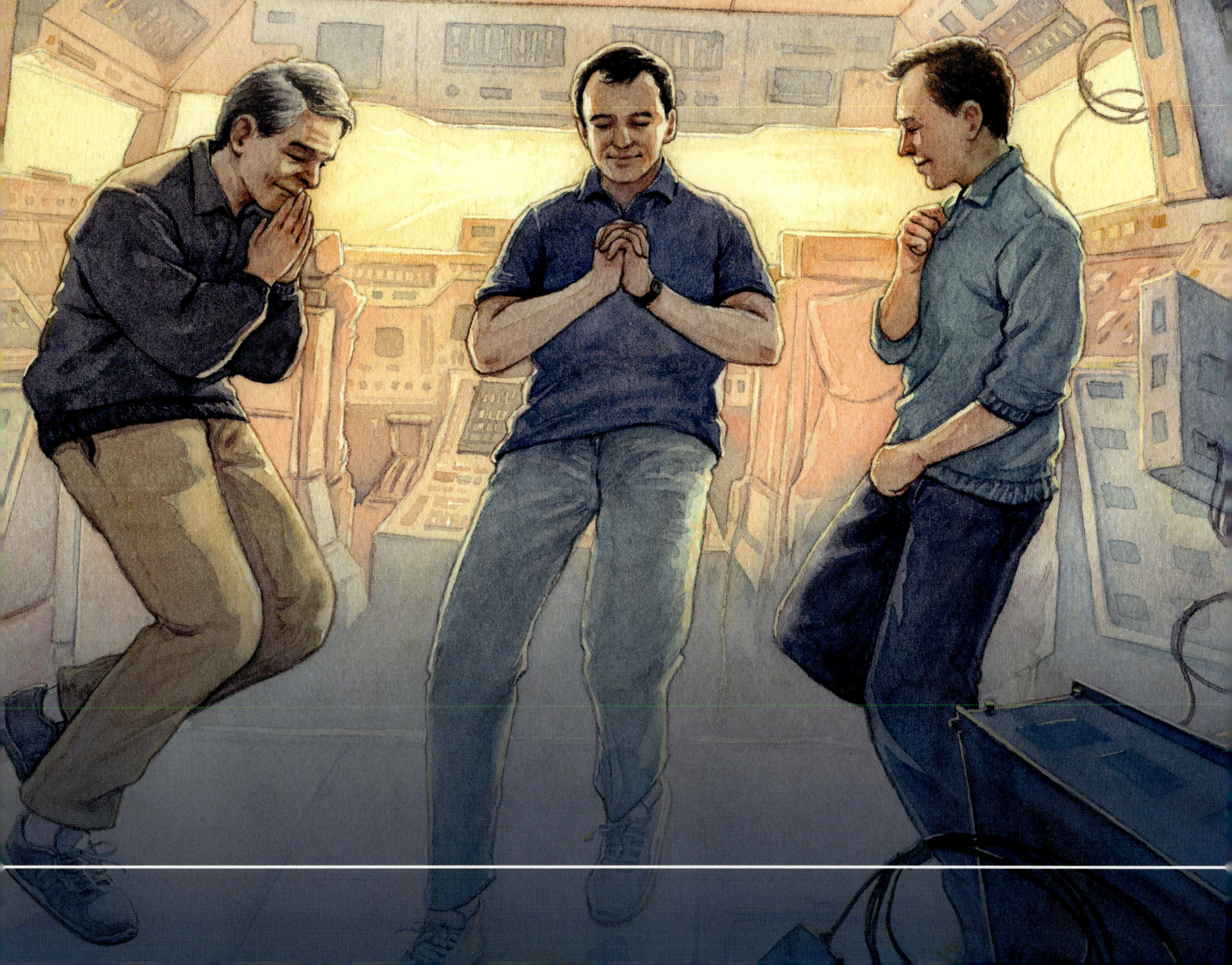

As Tom was praying, he floated over to a window. He saw the Earth, big, beautiful, and filling half the sky in the window. Tom thought about his family, who had gone to church and received Jesus in Communion. He thought of the billions of people who lived on Earth and about how much God loved every single one of them. Tom prayed that each of them would know that God was caring for them, just like he was caring for Tom in space.

After their time of prayer, the astronauts got back to work. They completed their science mission in eleven days and landed safely back on Earth.

APRIL 19, 1994: The landing of STS-59 is delayed one day due to weather.

When they touched down in the California desert, Tom prayed, "Thank you, Jesus, for our success on this mission. You've been with me in space. You've been with me on Earth. You're always with me. I'll never forget the gift of your love!"

APRIL 20, 1994, at 9:54 a.m. (PDT): The crew of STS-59 aboard *Endeavour* safely lands at Edwards Air Force Base in California.

Hello to all young readers and explorers!

I'm so happy to share my space story with you. Perhaps you'll be taking your own trips to space one day. Maybe you will search for life on Mars or mine an asteroid. Wherever you go, and whatever you do, God will be going with you. My crewmates and I on the shuttle *Endeavour* were so blessed to take Jesus in the Eucharist with us into space. He'll be with you as well—whenever and wherever you need him. Knowing God was with me on my space journeys helped me succeed in my work as an astronaut, exploring this tremendous universe. As you journey through life on and off our Spaceship Earth, receive Communion at Mass and take Jesus along in your heart. With God at your side, there's no fear—only wonder and gratitude for what he's given us.

God bless you and keep exploring!

Astronaut Tom Jones

Astronauts included in the STS-59 crew portrait include (standing in rear, left to right) Kevin P. Chilton, pilot; and Sidney M. Gutierrez, commander. Seated left to right are Linda M. Godwin, payload commander; and mission specialists Thomas D. Jones, Jay Apt, and Michael R. Clifford. Launched aboard the Space Shuttle *Endeavour* on April 9, 1994 at 7:05:00 am (EDT), the STS-59 mission deployed the Space Radar Laboratory (SRL-1).

Liftoff of the *Endeavour* on April 9, 1994

Astronaut Tom inside the *Endeavour*

Onboard portrait of crew: Astronaut Sidney M. Gutierrez, mission commander (front center) is flanked by astronauts Jerome (Jay) Apt and Thomas D. Jones, both mission specialists. On the back row are (left to right) astronaut Kevin P. Chilton, pilot; Linda M. Godwin, payload commander; and Michael R. (Rich) Clifford, mission specialist

A radar image of the Kilauea volcano in Hawaii taken during the STS-59 mission. Lava flows from 100 years ago can be seen, even where they are now covered by forests. This helps scientists predict where lava will go in future eruptions.

Astronaut Tom eating a meal on middeck of the *Endeavour*

View of STS-59 *Endeavour's* payload bay featuring Space Radar Laboratory

The Space Shuttle *Endeavour* landing at Edwards Air Force Base, California

Astronaut Tom anchored to bunk facility while working on a computer

Astronaut Tom, mission specialist, monitors cameras as the *Endeavour* orbits the Earth

More to Know . . .

What is the Eucharist?

"This is my body, given up for you." "This is my blood, given up for you."

Jesus said these words at the Last Supper when he gave us the gift of the Eucharist. At Mass, the priest says these same words. It is like all of us are at the table with Jesus.

These words are called "the Words of Institution." When the priest says them, the bread and wine in his hands become the Body and Blood of Jesus. The Eucharist is the Body and Blood of Jesus. It is no longer bread and wine, even though it still looks and tastes like bread and wine. In the Eucharist, Jesus is truly present with us!

When Catholics receive the Eucharist, it is called "Holy Communion." Whether you receive one big piece of the Precious Body of Jesus or one tiny drop of his Precious Blood, you are receiving all of Jesus.

The Eucharist is also called "The Most Blessed Sacrament," because it is the best gift that God could have given us. It is the gift of himself! Thank you, Jesus, for this amazing gift.

Who can receive the Eucharist?

You can receive Holy Communion if you are a baptized Catholic and you understand that it is truly Jesus. You must also be free of serious sin. (Serious sin can be forgiven in the Sacrament of Penance.) We do not eat or drink for one hour before we receive the Eucharist.

What is an Extraordinary Minister of Holy Communion?

Priests and deacons are the people who usually distribute Holy Communion at Mass. (They are the Ordinary Ministers.) But sometimes they need help! There might be a lot of people at Mass or someone might not be able to come to Mass because they are sick (or in space). They need someone to bring them Jesus in the Eucharist.

There are certain adults who are chosen by their pastors to be "Extraordinary Ministers of Holy Communion." They receive training about how to respectfully give Holy Communion to people.

Astronaut Kevin Chilton was an Extraordinary Minister of Holy Communion who brought the Eucharist aboard the space shuttle *Endeavour* and gave Holy Communion to Astronauts Tom Jones and Sidney Gutierrez on April 17, 1994.

How is the Eucharist stored?

The Eucharist really is the Body and Blood of Jesus! It is not treated like other food.

After Mass, the priests, deacons, and Extraordinary Ministers of Holy Communion consume all of the Precious Blood of Jesus. They either consume all of the Precious Body or they can store it for bringing Holy Communion to the sick.

The special container that the Precious Body is stored in is called a ciborium. The ciborium is placed in a box in the church or chapel. The box is called a tabernacle. A candle, called a sanctuary lamp, is lit to show that Jesus is truly present in the tabernacle.

When priests, deacons, or Extraordinary Ministers of Holy Communion bring the Eucharist to someone outside of Mass, they use a special container called a pyx (pronounced "picks").

Astronaut Kevin Chilton used a pyx to bring the Eucharist into space.

What is Eucharistic Adoration?

Many people like to pray in front of Jesus in the Eucharist. This is called "Eucharistic Adoration."

You can adore Jesus in the Eucharist every time you go into a Catholic church. Jesus is present in the Eucharist in the tabernacle. Just look for a lit candle to remind you that he is really there!

Sometimes, Jesus in the Eucharist is put in a special stand called a monstrance. This is called "Exposition" because the Eucharist is exposed so you can see the Precious Body of Jesus.

The Eucharist really is Jesus! So, at Eucharistic Adoration you are actually looking at God himself. This helps us to remember that God really is always with us.

About the Author

Cecilia Cicone is from Delaware. She and her dog, Rocco, can be found driving around in her pickup truck and teaching people about God's love. In her free time, she enjoys reading and sharing true stories that remind people that God is always with us.

About the Illustrator

Gabhor Utomo was born in Indonesia. He moved to California to pursue his passion in art. He received his degree from the Academy of Art University in San Francisco in spring 2003. Since his graduation he has worked as a freelance illustrator and has illustrated a number of children's books. His first children's book, *Kai's Journey to Gold Mountain*, is a story about a young Chinese immigrant on Angel Island.

Gabhor's works have won numerous awards from local and national art organizations. His painting of Senator Milton Marks is in a permanent collection at the California State Building in downtown San Francisco.

Gabhor lives with his wife Dina and his twin girls in Portland, Oregon.

To review more of Gabhor's work online, please visit: www.gabhorutomo.com.

Pauline

Who are the Daughters of St. Paul?

We are Catholic sisters with a mission. Our task is to bring the love of Jesus to everyone like Saint Paul did. You can find us in over 50 countries. Our founder, Blessed James Alberione, showed us how to reach out to the world through the media. That's why we publish books, make movies and apps, record music, broadcast on radio, perform concerts, help people at our bookstores, visit parishes, use social media and the Internet, and pray for all of you.